AN AKA DETECTIVE CLUB MYSTERY

AKA

THE MYSTERY OF THE MISSING GEOMETRY BOXES

VIDYA V.

Illustrations by
CHARBAK DIPTA

SCHOLASTIC
New York Toronto London Auckland
Sydney New Delhi Hong Kong

Dedicated to my father, Raj Varadarajan, who has been waiting to read my books since 1984.

Dad: 'You have a way with words. You will probably be a writer.'

Me (age 8): 'Will not!'

Published by Scholastic India Pvt. Ltd.
A subsidiary of Scholastic Inc., New York, 10012 (USA).
Publishers since 1920, with international operations in Canada, Australia, New Zealand, the United Kingdom, India, and Hong Kong.

For information regarding permission, write to:
Scholastic India Pvt. Ltd.
A-27, Ground Floor, Sigma Centre
Infocity-1, Sector 34, Gurgaon-122001 (India)

First edition: September 2024

ISBN-13: 978-93-5954-156-3

Printed in India at Shree Maitrey Printech Pvt. Ltd., Noida

Contents

DETECTIVES, ASSEMBLE! 5

YES, GEOMETRY BOXES 11

FOLLOW THE DATA 17

THE TINY NINJA SPY 24

SIDEY CYCLE 31

BACKPEDALLING 36

FOLLOWING THE BOXES 40

ANOTHER ANGLE 44

FAMILY TIES…TRIES 49

A PUZZLE WITHIN A PUZZLE 54

TECH TO THE RESCUE 59

ASHA STRIKES AGAIN 62

AN UN-GENIUS MOVE 64

GOING…NOWHERE 70

THE WAITING 77

NOT AN ACCIDENT 82

AARAV THINKS FAST 87

IT'S STILL OUT THERE 92

SKILL LEVEL: 1, TIME: NIL 95

SLEDGEHAMMERED 101

A STEP BACK 105

A STEP FORWARD 108

ASHA'S EPIPHANY 113

NUGGETS IS...CHICKEN 118

BUT WHERE'S THE PROOF? 122

SECOND CHANCES 126

MR NOT-SO-PERFECT 130

ACKNOWLEDGEMENTS 134

ABOUT THE AUTHOR 136

CHAPTER 1

DETECTIVES, ASSEMBLE!

'...we pray for courage and humiliteeeee...
That-we-may-see-with-clariteeeee...
To keep a sharp mind,
And approach all learning in KIND!

So that all may know and seeeeee...
Learning is Everything! Learning is EVERYTHING!'

The assembly prayer ended on its usual booming note, as students fidgeted and kicked up dust.

It had been almost a month since they solved their last (and first) case. And the AKA detectives (Asha, Karthik, and Aarav or Aarav, Karthik, and Asha depending on who was explaining the name), were as restless as the rest of the students, though for entirely different reasons.

'and I do not know what it says about our school, when day after day, I receive complaints about personal items going missing!'

Asha, the youngest at nine, was, of course, the least fidgety. One, because she was standing at the very front of class four right under the principal's nose, being the shortest in her class. And two, because she was one of those kids who paid attention in class. She was

now listening intently to the principal, who had finished reading his morning notices and was gleefully taking a few minutes to vent.

Thirteen-year-old Karthik, the second member of the gang (regardless of who was saying it) was gazing up into space. To the untrained eye, it would seem that he was daydreaming, but Aarav who was watching him surreptitiously from his class line, knew better. Aarav's sister Asha was book smart, but Karthik was smart-smart. He was probably looking at those loud speakers carrying the principal's words back to them and wondering how to hack it. And chances were, if Karthik put his mind to it, he could probably do it.

'Geometry boxes! Seven of them! In one day! Do we have geometry box collectors in this school? Are you reselling? How cheap can students become if they have to steal, not one, not two…but seven geometry boxes this month?'

Aarav grinned as he imagined Karthik replacing words in the principal's rant with bad words. He shook his head and toed more dust up from the ground. They'd probably get caught. After solving their first case, **The Mystery of the Graveyard Gold**, two months ago, the trio had become extremely popular in school. Both amongst the students and the teachers. Karthik who had been trying to keep his brains under the radar, now found himself a bit of a superstar in school.

And why not, thought Aarav, scuffing more dirt and watching his white shoes turn red. *He was just rich before. Now they know he's smart too.*

Aarav who was a year younger than Karthik at twelve years, tried not to feel too resentful. Karthik was, after all, now one of his best friends. And Aarav had also received his fair share of attention for being the one to finally crack the Graveyard Gold case wide open.

But sadly, that sheen seemed to have faded, and his teachers were back to clucking their tongues over his marks. Even worse, now his papers were being returned with remarks like, '*...if you were smart enough to solve cases that had the CBI fooled for years...*' or snide encouragement as he stood at the board and stared at mystifying algebra equations '*C'mon Aarav, it's easier than solving a crime!*' while sniggers erupted behind him. Aarav was beginning to think the fame wasn't worth it.

Especially if he couldn't prove he could do it again.

That was the problem, for all three of them. One-case-solved detectives weren't really detectives, but just lucky kids. They needed another win. And for that...they needed another case. Any case would do.

✧

'Any case will not do, Aarav as I've told you before.' Karthik slurped his cola and leaned back in his chair, oblivious to a group of class nine girls eyeing him from the next table.

'It has to be equal or better.'

'Besides we have a case!' chimed in Asha, looking up from her textbook, pencil poised in the air. Asha had started joining them, grudgingly, in the canteen during their one common break as long as she was allowed to 'finish' her work. By finish she meant solving problems from the Olympiad Maths textbook.

'The Mystery of the Missing Geometry Boxes,' she intoned.

The all-girls table behind them burst into laughter. Aarav turned red. Karthik rolled his eyes and lowered his voice. 'Do you think that's equal or better than gold?' he muttered addressing the top of Asha's oiled hair. As always, Asha could ignore everything and everybody if she had problems to solve.

'I think two missing geometry boxes is carelessness, four is theft, but seven is a mystery,' retorted Asha's head.

'Let's discuss this somewhere more private?' Aarav replied glancing back at the other table.

'Ignore them!' Karthik and Asha chimed in together.

Aarav flushed and then leaned forward angrily. 'We cannot be detectives if everyone knows what we are up to. Detectives work quietly in the background. Not in full view of the school!'

He sat back with a thump.

'I agree with that,' said Karthik, his brows raised. 'And so by that reasoning, we cannot solve our next mystery in school. I vote "no" to missing geometry boxes.'

Aarav nodded. 'No geometry boxes.'

Asha slumped. 'Fine.'

CHAPTER 2

YES, GEOMETRY BOXES

'...and Ramesh uncle's brother's missing dog turned up yesterday, so that's out, too,' Aarav finished reciting.

They were back in their new and improved clubhouse. Disguised on the outside as a huge black plastic water tank, the clubhouse was perched on the highest part of the Cambridge Venetia apartment complex. To reach it, you had to take the elevator to the top floor, and then wander to the furthest edge of the terrace. There you'd see a grill gate behind which the maintenance staff stored disused objects and rubbish, that no apartment association ever felt the need to get rid of.

And while any kid could easily squeeze themselves through the bent gates, most would only notice the dusty piles of broken junk. Unless you knew where to look. Up.

In one corner of this terrace was a hole in the roof, with a cleverly hidden rope ladder, which the team used to reach their clubhouse (and which could also be pulled up to avoid unexpected visitors when meetings were in session).

The clubhouse itself was a huge, yet empty plastic water tank with a large door flap cut into the plastic. Inside the clubhouse were some of the gadgets that had originally been Karthik's, before he befriended Aarav and Asha. After the clubhouse was ransacked during their last case, each of the members had contributed something, making the clubhouse feel like it now belonged to all of them.

They were gathered around the table, watching as Aarav ripped the potential mystery cases off their battered and reclaimed noticeboard, and chucked them in the bin.

Gloomily, they stared at the blank board.

'This won't do. Without a mystery, we aren't different from any other group of friends, just hanging out!' said Karthik.

'That's not true, they don't have a secret clubhouse like us,' Asha said, rummaging in her backpack.

'But what's the point of a secret clubhouse?' retorted Karthik. 'When we haven't had another case in a whole two months?'

'Hey, let's relax...' chimed in Aarav. 'We all want to solve a case. Just because there's no case–'

'There is a case!' shouted Asha. 'The Mystery of the Missing Geometry–'

'NO GEOMETRY BOXES' shouted Aarav and Karthik back.

'Asha, you keep pushing...' Aarav shook his head.

'Because you both are idiots! You!' she turned angrily to face Karthik, 'only want the prestigious cases. We got lucky the first time, not everything will be as exciting as gold! Don't real detectives spend boring hours on stakeouts and research? Do they say, "It's too boring, I can't do it"?'

'And you!' Asha swivelled a bit too rapidly towards Aarav and banged her elbow on the table. 'You think geometry boxes are just being nicked by other kids!' she ground out, eyes watering as she rubbed her elbow.

'They are!'

'From three schools?' Asha glared.

Aarav and Karthik exchanged startled looks.

'That's right, if you both had even bothered to check, as I did...you would know geometry boxes are not just being stolen from Anthony's, but also from Shree Mandir and Holy Trinity!' she ended, naming the two other schools in their neighbourhood.

The boys sat in silence.

'How do you know that?' Karthik asked quietly.

'I asked!' Asha's glasses flashed. 'And I didn't have to go far to ask either. Kids from our apartment go to all these schools. Their teachers are all complaining.'

'And how many geometry boxes have been stolen so far?' Aarav asked.

'Twenty-seven as far as I can tell,' said Asha pulling out a notebook. She flipped the pages. 'Seven from our school, eight from Shree Mandir and twelve from Trinity. And I haven't even asked all the kids yet.'

She tossed the notebook on the table and leaned back, while Karthik and Aarav examined her notes.

It looked like this:

Name: Jayshree H, Apt: 345 D, School: Shree Mandir, Lost: 1 geometry box

Name: Rakshika MN, Apt: 128 A, School: Trinity, Lost: 1 geometry box

Name: Shreekesh Mukthinath, Apt: 242 A, School: Shree Mandir, Lost: 1 geometry box

Name: Sarah Jonathan, Apt: 203 D, School: Trinity, Lost: 1 geometry box

Name: Yohaan Mathews, Apt: 011 B, School: Trinity, Lost: 1 geometry box

Name: John Parker, Apt: 142 A, School: Anthony's,
Lost: 1 geometry box

Name: Arjun JP, Apt: 142 D, School: Anthony's,
Lost: 1 geometry box

Name: Preethi Mathews, Apt: 021 C, School: Anthony's,
Lost: 1 geometry box

Name: Manjunath M, Apt: 221 D, School: Shree Mandir,
Lost: 1 geometry box

'This is good work, Asha,' muttered Aarav. Karthik nodded, biting his lip. He looked at Aarav.

'I guess we have a new case.'

Asha beamed.

'It's good work,' agreed Karthik waving Asha's notebook at her, 'but incomplete.'

'What? I–'

Karthik held up a hand. 'I know! I know! We didn't help you, and that's our mistake. This is good data. But you never asked anyone whether their boxes were new or old. Or which brand? And the date on which they lost it.'

Asha frowned. 'You're right, with all that we could detect some patterns.'

Aarav scratched his head. 'You mean like if they were all stolen on the same day? We know that didn't happen.'

Karthik sat back down at the table. 'No, but what if they all happened on a Monday? Or during the weekends only?'

'But weekends only, would mean…it didn't happen at school,' stated Aarav slowly.

'Exactly!' grinned Karthik. 'We need more data.'

'So we can find a pattern,' added Asha.

'And use the results to lead us to our thief!' Aarav concluded.

Karthik grinned at the siblings who were grinning back at him.

'Let's get to it.'

CHAPTER 3

FOLLOW THE DATA

It had been a trying week and the trio was exhausted. What began as a simple survey rapidly became an uphill task.

Cambridge Venetia was a huge apartment in the Cambridge Layout area of Bengaluru. Located between three schools, this aged complex originally had only four blocks (A, B, C, D) but had later expanded into the common green area by adding smaller blocks E and F, before the association committee took over and kicked the builders out.

The end result was that the apartment complex had six blocks across six floors, with four to eight apartments on each floor depending on the block. This turned out to be an easy maths problem for Karthik, a complex social adventure for Asha, and a pounding headache for Aarav.

Most of the apartment kids still didn't like Karthik, and refused to talk to him. So he stopped knocking on doors.

Then, the moms started getting angry at the disturbance (particularly post-lunch hours) and even angrier when reminded about how many geometry boxes were being stolen/replaced.

And *then*, word got out that they were trying to solve the case.

Some of the older kids thought it was hilarious to say they lost five or six geometry boxes, and made up the dates on which they were lost.

Asha would seethe, and start spewing legal quotes with words like 'false testimony' and 'fabrication of evidence'. After this happened a few times, Aarav learnt to start hustling her out of the door before she reached the words 'punished with imprisonment of up to seven years'.

Every evening, Asha and Aarav would then bring whatever information they had collected to Karthik in the clubhouse. Karthik would enter the answers into an Excel spreadsheet on their new/old computer.

'What a colossal waste of time!' groaned Aarav. Karthik who was still typing in the last few entries did not respond. 'Why are you still entering those answers? Those idiots in D Block were the biggest jokers of the lot.'

Karthik swivelled to face them. Both Asha and Aarav were sprawled bonelessly in their chairs. He rolled his way to the banged-up mini fridge, and pulled out two colas, and a fruit juice.

The first time Karthik offered Asha a cola, she indignantly stated that even a single serving of cola would increase her sugar intake over the WHO permissible limits.

Karthik handed Asha her juice, which their fridge now stocked especially for her.

'Do you remember me asking you to mark the answers that you thought were from those idiots?' he asked her now.

Asha glared back through her thick spectacles. 'I remember also asking you WHY. And I also remember you not answering. Just assume I remember everything.'

Also irritated, Aarav grabbed his cola from Karthik's hand. 'Do you want to tell us, or keep us in suspense?'

Unruffled, Karthik turned back to the screen and tilted it towards them. 'Those lines marked in yellow are from the jokers. I'm going to remove them as we are assuming their answers are nonsense.' Karthik started working as he continued to speak.

'Next, I'm going to highlight the answers of those who didn't go to one of our neighbouring schools.'

'They aren't that many,' said Aarav, now peering over his shoulder.

'And they didn't lose any boxes,' added Asha, her eyes closed as she sipped her drink.

'Correct. Let's take them out as well. Now look at what we have left.' Karthik did something and a table opened up on a new page of their spreadsheet.

'It's called a pivot table. We can now look at how many boxes were lost in each school.'

SCHOOLS	COUNT OF LOST
Anthony's	16 (YUGA)
Shree Mandir	13 (YUGA)
Trinity	18 (YUGA)

'That's a lot of geometry boxes…'

'Yes, and they're all…'

'Yuga brand!'

'Already knew that…' added Asha with eyes still closed.

'And here's the timeline of the thefts,' added Karthik.

'The first theft took place last month…and the latest one was…' Aarav traced his finger along the timeline.

'Two days ago. Nothing reported since then.'

'And nothing was reported lost over the weekend.'

'So we have a school thief?'

'I think it's safe to assume that.'

'I don't agree.' The boys turned to look at Asha. She opened her eyes and sat up.

'Kids only look for their geometry box when they have homework or when they have class. That's when they *noticed* the boxes went missing. Classes don't happen on the weekends and while I do my homework on the weekends…' she paused significantly.

'Hardly anyone else does!' finished Aarav with another groan. 'She's right. We've completely wasted our time.' He threw his notebook on the table and fell back into his chair.

Karthik stared thoughtfully at them both. 'Hmm... I think you are right, but I don't think we wasted our time. Because we've learnt something.' He stood up and strode to their notice board.

'Geometry boxes are being stolen, but from *only* three schools in our neighbourhood. And only kids who have bought Yuga geometry boxes are being robbed,' Karthik finished writing on the whiteboard which was half of their notice board and turned back to his friends.

'That's not much,' commented Asha. 'Why are you smiling?' added Aarav grumpily.

'Because,' Karthik said still grinning, 'it's really a mystery! I wasn't convinced until now. Look, only three schools, Yuga brand. Forty-seven geometry boxes! Who steals like that? We have a thief in our neighbourhood and he's looking for something! What could that be?'

'Acute angles?' Aarav said sourly.

Karthik was undeterred. 'I think we should investigate the factory that makes the boxes. And all the shops from where everyone bought the boxes.'

'I'm not going around the apartments asking again!'

'We don't have to,' said Asha gurgling the bottom of her juice box. 'There are only two places in our neighbourhood for school supplies, Kamakshi Kadai and our very own school bookshop.' She lobbed the empty carton straight at the dustbin and missed.

Karthik nodded, 'Alright we'll start there.'

As they filed out of the clubhouse, he muttered to Aarav, 'I just hope your sister's detective skills are better than her aim.'

CHAPTER 4

THE TINY NINJA SPY

Asha was (of course) right.

A Google search brought up the factory website which made Yuga brand's geometry boxes. Karthik was surprised to learn that they were manufactured on the outskirts of Bengaluru, in Peenya. A quick call by Aarav (who could speak passable Kannada and pretended to be a shop owner who wanted to distribute school supplies), confirmed it. Only six shops in Bengaluru sold Yuga brand, and two of these (Kamakshi Kadai, and their school bookshop) were the only ones in their neighbourhood.

'And apparently, if I sell geometry boxes I won't have much competition, and should turn a profit in Q3, whatever that means,' finished Aarav shaking his head.

'Well if our detective club doesn't take off, we can consider it,' responded Karthik in all seriousness.

'Could that be a reason?' ventured Asha cautiously. 'Profits, as everyone buys more than one?'

Karthik shrugged. 'It seems unlikely. Geometry boxes don't really cost more than ₹100 each.'

'And why start only now?' Aarav piped up. 'They would have to steal year after year to make any money, right?' Aarav turned to their maths whiz Karthik for confirmation, who nodded.

'If a shop sold fifty geometry boxes, and then sold another fifty, then at best...100 boxes at ₹100 each would give them ₹10,000. But the shops pay manufacturing costs, too.'

Aarav's brain, which had automatically disengaged when he heard what sounded like a maths statement problem, suddenly snapped back to attention. 'What's that?'

'Like 50 per cent of the cost. For a set of 100 boxes, they would have paid ₹5000. And when they sell, they make the money they invested, plus another ₹5000.' Karthik shrugged. 'I don't see the culprit being the shopkeepers, but we will know when we talk to them.'

✧

The next day, Asha entered the school bookshop after her classes were over. They had decided she would have the best opportunity to question Shop Uncle (as the shop owner was commonly called), as junior classes ended an hour earlier than the rest of the school. This would also give Asha the opportunity to investigate the bookshop without its usual crowd of middle and senior kids frantically buying pencils, pens, badges and replacement notebooks before the next bell.

'Also, no one would suspect that our tiny nine-year-old is capable of spy-level interrogation techniques.' Karthik had added, though not within Asha's hearing, Aarav noticed.

Inside the small shop, Asha hung back from the counter and pretended to examine a display of notebooks as she waited for the parent of a nursery child to finish their purchases.

'Yes dear?'

Asha turned and smiled at the shopkeeper.

Karthik would've been astounded to see the change in her face. She tilted her head, widened her eyes and gave him a blank look. She came as close as she could to the counter, forcing Shop Uncle to lean over to regard her.

'*Sollu ma…mummy engai?*'

In a sweet voice (which usually worked on her Appa, but caused her mother to raise her eyebrows suspiciously), Asha said, 'Mummy is outside. She asked me to get a geo–, geomit…'

'Geometry box?' Shop Uncle smiled down at her helpfully.

'Yes uncle! Geomilitary box. For anna. He keeps losing it!' she added with the louder confidence of someone parroting her mother's words.

'Ahhh… I know. There's a thief! Many are losing their geometry boxes.' He moved towards the back of the shop and began to rummage in a cardboard box in the back. 'I've told Principal Sir.'

'Why is it back there, uncle?' Asha queried pointing to the back of the shop.

'Because they are getting stolen so often, *chellam*. I haven't lost any, but just to be safe.'

'How many are in that box? One lakh?' she added innocently.

Shop Uncle guffawed loudly, and leaned down to pinch her cheek. Asha froze as she battled all her primal instincts. 'Only one hundred, *ma*. They come in boxes of 100.'

He carried the Yuga geometry box to his register book and started writing.

'What are you writing uncle?' Asha chirped, holding up a crisp, 100-rupee note.

'I'm writing the accounts, dear. I write for everything sold. Sometimes it's crowded and I don't have time, but for the geometry boxes, I told Principal Sir, I would keep a separate record.'

'So many geometry boxes have been sold?' Asha got up on her tiptoes and tried to look at his notes. Smiling indulgently, he showed her the page from the register book:

DATE	NAME	CLASS	AMOUNT
3/9/2024	Priya S.	8 C	100
5/9/2024	Rachel Sudhir	9 A	100
6/9/2024	Aaditya Nair	7 A	100
10/9/2024	Dev Krishnan	6 B	80
10/9/2024	Karthik Sooraj	7 C	80
12/9/2024	Siddharth TY	8 A	80
13/9/2024	Raj Reddy	8 D	80
14/9/2024	Jason Parker	7 C	80

'You see, I'm offering discounts now, because poor children have to buy twice. It's not easy for all parents to keep buying. I should know, I raised two sons myself. My youngest, Ayyapan, is in this school only. 9B. Maybe you know him?'

Asha shook her head.

'He's been studying very well this year. First ranker. He helps me after school with deliveries.' Shop Uncle put the book away. 'My eldest runs a printing press! See he makes these calendars for me,' he added waving to the wall of a large glossy print of a bulbul perched amongst gulmohar flowers, below which was a grid for the month of September.

Taking her money, he opened his cash box. 'Greedy fellow must be selling all those boxes. What will the students do?' Still shaking his head and making clucking noises, he handed her ₹20 back.

'Thank you uncle!' Asha simpered.

'You're welcome, dear. And tell Amma not to scold anna too much. Many are losing and buying. Principal Sir will catch them.'

Not if we catch him first, thought Asha grimly, as she exited the shop.

CHAPTER 5

SIDEY CYCLE

Later that day, Aarav had a similar, if somewhat less nauseating, conversation with the Kamakshi Kadai owner, who had also started giving discounts. 'So we know it's not the shopkeepers themselves,' he concluded.

Asha and Karthik both nodded in silent agreement, deep in thought. Aarav, miffed that he was again the last to reach a known conclusion, added grumpily, 'Now what?'

Karthik ran his hands through his hair. 'I'm stumped.' He looked towards Asha.

'How about those CCTV cameras in school?' asked Asha.

'They are only around the main office building, and parking areas.' Karthik replied. 'That's primary, admin and staff. It's unlikely there are many geometry boxes there. The other ones cover the "in" and "out" gates. Even if the thief is among them, they aren't likely to be holding it in view, right?'

'What about that Sidey Cycle!' exclaimed Aarav. 'He might know.' Surprised, Karthik nodded thoughtfully. 'That's a good idea. I forgot about Sidey.'

'Who's Sidey?' Asha asked.

'He's a cycle vendor, who stands down the road from our school. Selling stuff,' muttered Aarav.

'What stuff?'

'Just stuff, Asha, leave it!'

'Gutka packets. Cigarettes.' Karthik interrupted. 'Lighters.' He continued ignoring Asha's gasp. 'And sometimes...'

'Stolen stuff,' finished Aarav.

'And how do you know this Sidey uncle?' Asha turned accusingly to Aarav.

'First of all, he's not Sidey UNCLE. He's just Sidey Cycle. And second of all, everyone knows after primary. There are always some in class, who buy.'

'Cigarettes?'

'You can sell stuff to him, too,' mused Karthik.

'And how do YOU know that!' Asha vented in his direction.

'I've sold small stuff to him when I needed cash. Watches. Ashtrays.' Karthik shrugged indifferently.

Asha and Aarav goggled.

'You sold stuff to HIM?'

'Why would YOU need cash?'

'Anyway,' Karthik continued, ignoring both questions. 'He's our local black market. If anyone was reselling stolen geometry boxes, Sidey would know.' He nodded decisively. 'Aarav, you need to talk to him tomorrow.'

'What? Why me? No way!'

'He knows me already.'

'Exactly, and it's your turn. I already spoke to the factory and Kamakshi Kadai. Asha spoke to Shop Uncle, and we've been doing the interviews. It's your turn!'

'It's not about that,' retorted Karthik frustratedly. 'Sidey is as sidey as they come. He's very cautious with me, because I'm a seller. He's all salesman with new boys, as he knows they are after the cigarettes.'

'So?'

'So, all those nervous kids always buy something *else* first. Some junk. Because they don't want to ask for cigarettes up front. Sidey sells two or three times, to the most nervous ones, before offering cigarettes.' Karthik chortled. 'It's a clever con.'

'The sale of tobacco and related products is prohibited within 100 yards of any educational institution...' Asha began.

'And you want me to be conned?' Aarav interrupted angrily. 'What if my parents or my mom's friends see me?'

'He's a cycle vendor. No one will care.'

'Of course, they'll care! I got in trouble just a month ago, for riding my bike down the Ulsoor Road. My dad's friends were out walking early, and promptly called my dad, who promptly took my bike away for a week. I'm not risking it.' Aarav folded his hands and sat back.

Karthik looked intrigued. 'How did your dad's friend recognize you whizzing by?'

Aarav looked blank.

'Uh...because they SAW him? They come home for dinner sometimes. Or we go to their homes. So obviously they know him. Loser.' Asha muttered.

'Well, lucky you. Not all of us have such perfect lives.' Karthik snapped back.

'Hey!' Aarav realized their conversation was getting out of hand, but before he could figure out what to do, Karthik angrily made a cutting motion with his hand. 'Sidey is our only next point of investigation. Unless you two have another idea?' They shook their heads.

'He knows me, and won't tell me what he's selling, only ask what I'm selling.' He turned towards Aarav, 'Unless you want your BABY sister to go asking for cigarettes, I suggest you approach him tomorrow.'

With that, Karthik grabbed his bag and exited the clubhouse, attempting to slam the flap behind him. It only sent a gust of air inside, scattering all their papers off the table.

It had been a long time since Aarav had seen Asha look as confused as he was.

'What was that all about?'

CHAPTER 6

BACKPEDALLING

The next day, Karthik continued the conversation as if nothing had happened. Aarav who had already resigned himself to talking to Sidey Cycle, was mildly surprised.

The previous night, while discussing strategies to approach Sidey, he and Asha wondered what they would do if Karthik decided to leave the club. Luckily, either Karthik had forgotten his flash of anger, or was pretending it didn't happen.

Either way, Aarav was relieved. He didn't want to think about what would happen to their case (and the AKA club) if they all started fighting.

'Just be yourself,' Karthik had muttered, as they approached the school corner around which Sidey was usually parked. 'Speak to him in Tamil or Kannada…'

Aarav nodded, his lips pressed tightly together. He hadn't felt this nervous since the day he had to read the news during the school prayer last year. He had stuttered a lot then.

Shouldering his backpack higher, Aarav strolled around the corner, half hoping Sidey Cycle wasn't there, until he saw the familiar rusted *katta vandi* up on its stand, with large bags hanging from the handle bars and a huge wooden box perched on the back carrier, strapped on with thin strips of rubber from old cycle air tubes.

Sidey himself looked like he had stepped out of a really bad movie. He was wearing a full-sleeved button-down shirt, which was once red, but had faded through repeated washing to a truly horrendous magenta. His sleeves were rolled up high, and his buttons were all open to reveal a yellow in-shirt. Sidey's hair was long, well-oiled, and combed over. His hair tips were dyed blonde.

As he approached, Aarav could see Sidey wore a chunky gold watch, and earrings too. He was talking loudly on the phone, and waved Aarav impatiently away. Surprised, Aarav came to a halt, as Sidey's conversation continued.

'They are always looking for money from me. Even if I tell them my mother passed away last month, they say their mother, father, and elder brother all died in an accident yesterday.'

Sidey guffawed loudly, before noticing Aarav still standing there.

'*Irru ma kanne.*'

'Enna?' eyes cold, Sidey lowered his head and raised his shoulders at Aarav.

'Anna...' Aarav began.

'I don't have anything here for boys like you.' Sidey's eyes scraped Aarav rudely up and down, taking in everything from his backpack, to his watch and dusty-yet-untorn shoes.

'Anna, geometry box?' blurted Aarav before Sidey could resume his conversation.

'Geometry box ah? Do I look like a school supply shop? GET LOST!' Sidey made a violent gesture with his phone.

'No anna...I lost two of mine...can't ask for another...' even as he was talking, Aarav vaguely appreciated that his nervousness sounded just like a kid who was too afraid to ask his mother for money to buy a third geometry box.

'I haven't stolen any boxes!' shouted Sidey. Realizing people were beginning to stare, Aarav took a step back and tried one last time.

'No anna, I just wanted to know if you have a few extra...?'

'GET LOST!'

Aarav turned and fled.

CHAPTER 7

FOLLOWING THE BOXES

'Aarav for the last time, if your folks come to hear, tell them it was for our case!'

It had taken a good hour, a cola and two packets of chips for Aarav to relax after his disastrous conversation with Sidey Cycle. He silently vowed he would never even walk down that corner of the school (which luckily wasn't on his way home) again.

Karthik who had been watching the interaction from the other end of the street, had assured him, that no adults had paid any attention, and that Sidey was always shouting at some kid or the other. That way he could protest that he always chased kids away, when an angry parent accosted him.

'You might have warned me about that,' muttered Aarav.

'Sorry,' said Karthik, who didn't look sorry at all.

'What do we do now?' interrupted Asha. 'I don't think we've effectively interviewed Sidey.'

'Hey! It's not like I can pretend to be cute and two–' shouted Aarav.

'That's not the only thing I do!' said Asha, eyes cold behind her spectacles.

'OK, OK...let's all just chill. Sidey didn't pan out. But–' he held up a hand quickly over Aarav's dark expression, 'I don't think he knows any more than we do.'

Karthik held up another hand to halt Asha's protest. 'If you remember, he immediately said he didn't know anything about the *stolen* boxes.' Karthik looked meaningfully at the siblings before adding, 'As though he's been asked before.'

'He was probably the first suspect,' said Asha shrewdly.

'I agree.' Karthik nodded.

'Fine,' huffed Aarav. 'It's not him and we still don't know where the geometry boxes are going, much less who's stealing them. What now?'

'Let's bait the thief!' said Asha.

Karthik and Aarav looked at her blankly. She rolled her eyes and held up the Yuga geometry box she had bought in the school shop. 'Let's leave this out, and see who takes it.'

'How do we do that?' Aarav looked blank.

'How is easy. But, where?' Karthik pondered.

'We will have to try school first, as that's where most of them...apparently...' she added purposefully, 'go missing.'

'We could have a stake-out,' Aarav enthused. 'Some place where we could watch even with our classes.'

'We could use RFID technology!'

Aarav looked puzzled. But before he could even ask what's that, Asha, the walking-talking dictionary, blurted 'Radio Frequency Identification'.

Karthik nodded. 'It's what they use in shops,' he explained to Aarav. 'Those plastic tags, to keep clothes from being stolen? You place a tag on the object and with a tag reader you can know where it is, and even where it is being moved to.' Karthik's eyes gleamed with tech enthusiasm.

'And do you have a reader?' Aarav asked pointedly.

'No.' Karthik slumped.

'So stake-out?'

Asha and Karthik exchanged glances. 'Stake-out!' they agreed.

CHAPTER 8

ANOTHER ANGLE

The idea of the stake-out was simple enough. Leave the geometry box out and see who took it. But in a school of one thousand students and forty hyper vigilant staff, it proved far more difficult than expected.

Karthik tried leaving the box on his table throughout the class only to have a queue of ever-helpful girls reminding him to put it away, as there was a thief on the loose. By the sixth time this happened, exasperated, he handed the box to Aarav.

Aarav managed to keep the box out on an empty desk on the back bench where he sat, for two periods, until it came under the sharp eyes of his class teacher, who gave him a dressing down for being so careless and told him sternly to put it away.

Asha's class hadn't started using geometry boxes yet, so that was out.

✧

'Who knew it would be so hard to get things stolen?' grumbled Aarav.

They were again in the canteen with the troublesome Yuga geometry box on the table between them.

'The trouble is that everyone is being extra cautious now. We've had almost a month of geometry boxes being stolen, and now…nothing.'

Asha looked up from her notebook. 'But that doesn't mean the thief has stopped, does it?'

Aarav shrugged. 'Maybe he found what he was looking for?'

Karthik sighed and ran a hand through his hair. 'Which is what?'

'I dunno!' retorted Aarav. 'Why would anyone need more than one geometry box?'

'Because he–,' began Karthik.

'Or she!' chimed in Asha.

'Or she...' he continued 'is looking for a particular box! What if there was something special about just one box?'

'And the thief has to steal every box to find it?' Aarav threw his hands up in the air. 'I don't get it.'

'Let's assume one box has a special prize in it.' Karthik turned to Asha. 'You said Shop Uncle has them in boxes of a hundred, right?'

Asha nodded.

'Right. What if something special was in one of those hundred boxes? And–'

'And the thief traced that box to this neighbourhood, but didn't know which shop it was in,' completed Asha.

'Exactly! And all those boxes were sold! And so...', Karthik pondered.

'He is now stealing one by one and checking each!' Asha finished. 'But for what?' she stared frustratedly at the boys, who looked equally blank.

'We have another problem,' ventured Aarav cautiously. 'What if the thief found what he was looking for? He wouldn't need to steal anymore. How will we ever find him?'

'Look,' muttered Karthik. 'We need to follow a box getting stolen. That'll lead us to who is doing it, and then we can find out the reason behind it. I think we should try the RFID technology idea again. I could get a reader…'

'The thief could be long gone by then,' interrupted Asha. 'I think we need to first find what was unique about that batch of geometry boxes. And *that* will lead us to *who*. Maybe we need to look closer at the factory.'

'And I think this case has run its course,' Aarav butted in. 'Unless a geometry box is stolen in the next couple of days, I say we drop it.'

The trio stared at each other in silence.

'Well, it sounds like we each have a lead to follow,' declared Karthik.

He pointed to Asha. 'You study the boxes and see if you can find out what made this carton unique.'

He turned to Aarav, 'and you keep your ears open both at school and the apartment to see if anyone turns up complaining about another lost box.'

Aarav nodded.

Karthik looked thoughtful. 'And I'll see if I can get my hands on an RFID tag and reader.'

CHAPTER 9

FAMILY TIES...TRIES

Karthik let himself into his apartment using the key code his mother had installed when they first moved in. Dropping his bag on the sofa, he kicked off his shoes and headed to the kitchen.

His mom, who worked long hours in a large finance company, would not be home till after dinner.

Their cook had set their kitchen table with rotis and sabji, and a plate for Karthik. As he ate, Karthik pondered over how best to obtain an RFID reader.

Digging out his mobile, he browsed online for a suitable set. Looking at the distance range they would have to be for the reader to track the box (if it ever got stolen), Karthik estimated it would cost him between ₹3000 and ₹5000.

Unlike what everyone thought (Asha and Aarav included), Karthik did not have unlimited funds at his disposal, like some sort of *Richie Rich* character. When he wanted something, he approached a parent and asked for it. While he usually got it, it did not mean questions weren't asked.

So how was Karthik to explain the need for an RFID reader to his mom? Science project, maybe? Unfortunately, he had recently obtained a new keyboard from his mom on a similar pretext. (Their clubhouse keyboard had been destroyed during their last adventure.)

Picking up his mobile phone again, he called his dad's number.

'Hi Karthik!' Ramya, his dad's PA, answered his phone. 'Your dad is in a meeting right now, can I take a message?' she chirped.

'Um...no,' answered Karthik distractedly. 'How long is his meeting going to last?'

'About an hour more, I'd say,' replied Ramya. He could hear raised voices in the background. 'Maybe longer,' she added tiredly.

Karthik's dad was a hedge fund manager, who also led his own successful practice. His long working hours, and frequent trips around the globe, made him extremely hard to get hold of.

'I'll let him know you had called,' Ramya hung up.

Karthik sighed.

✧

Wearing her mother's slightly used hair-dye gloves, and armed with her eyebrow tweezers, Asha adjusted her glasses as scientifically as she could. Carefully, she used the tweezers to pick out the pencil from its receptacle and placed it on the clean, white sheet of paper next to her. Using her own steel ruler, Asha measured the pencil.

'One pencil, 4 inches in length,' she intoned.

Behind her, Aarav sighed. 'Do we really need to do it this way?'

Why had he been loitering in his room, when he could've been doing anything else, thought Aarav regretfully. Hastily he scribbled, 'pencil: 4 inches', in Asha's notebook, as she turned and glared at him.

'Forensic scientists,' she began loftily as she turned back to examine the open geometry box on her pristine table, 'analyse evidence from crime scenes to assist in investigations.'

'Eraser, 1.3 inches.'

Aarav gritted his teeth. He wrote it down.

'But we aren't forensic scientists. And that,' he pointed at the open geometry that Asha was painstakingly dissecting, 'is not from a crime scene!'

'Nevertheless,' Asha intoned, 'it's a good way to learn how to dissect and catalogue. What is this?' she asked holding up a plastic semicircle.

Aarav raised his eyebrows and tried not to smile. 'You don't know?'

Asha's eyes which were cold before, narrowed dangerously. Aarav held up both hands in surrender. 'It's a protractor…we use it to draw angles.'

'One protractor, 5.5 inches.'

Aarav sighed again and went back to writing.

✧

For the fourth time, Karthik called his dad's number only to hear the busy signal again. The first meeting had been followed by another meeting, followed by a call, which was still going on. It was past 10 p.m., and Karthik expected his mother to be back any time. He wanted to finish his call with his dad, before his mother came home and became suspicious.

Suddenly, his message notification pinged. It was his dad.

`Sorry, it's been a hectic day. Can we talk tomorrow?`

Desperately, he replied:

`Hi dad! Science project. Need this:` Karthik included a link to the product and held his breath.

His dad started typing...

`Will have it delivered tomorrow.` Karthik released his breath and grinned. Problem solved! Looking back at his phone, Karthik noticed his dad was still typing.

`Don't call me for unimportant things.`

CHAPTER 10

A PUZZLE WITHIN A PUZZLE

'I've got news!' Karthik dropped his bag in his chair and carefully sat down with his flimsy bowl of piping hot noodles. He glanced casually around the canteen and took note that they were relatively alone.

'So do we!' Asha looked unusually excited. Karthik looked suspiciously between the two of them. Aarav was grinning, too.

'OK, you go first.' He nodded to Asha.

Quietly, she slid a small rectangular coupon under Karthik's nose.

Karthik nodded. 'The Yuga Maths Puzzle entry ticket. There's one in every geometry box. Thinking of entering?'

Asha held up a hand to stop Aarav from interrupting.

'Notice anything *unusual* about this entry ticket?'

Karthik examined the ticket more carefully.

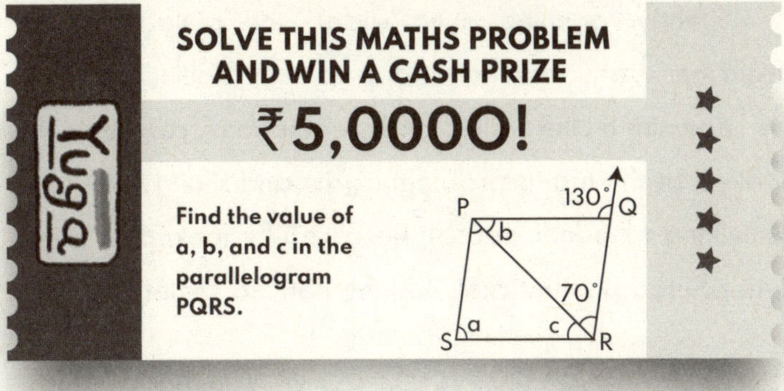

Every geometry box came with this smallish coupon, with a printed maths sum on it. You wrote the answer, entered your name, school, and other information, and then mailed your answer for prizes. In case of multiple correct entries, an answer would be picked at random like in a lottery. Karthik had never bothered entering, because the problems given on the coupon were easy and he knew enough about mathematical probability to know his chances of being picked were less than slim. He looked up at Asha. She and Aarav were now openly grinning at him. Puzzled, he looked back at the ticket again. An easy, 'find the angle' maths problem. Information boxes to fill up. Cash rewards. And the rules and regulations in a font size he could barely read.

'Give up?' Asha chirped.

Karthik scowled at her. 'Got a magnifying glass?'

Silently, grinning even wider, she pulled one out from her bag, and handed it to him. Rolling his eyes, he examined the rules and regulations carefully. He looked at the maths problem again and silently solved it. Unwilling to admit defeat, he carefully looked at every line printed on the ticket, until he noticed something odd:

CASH REWARD OF ₹5,OOOO!

'Is that an O instead of a zero?' Karthik looked back at Asha. She nodded.

'So…it's ₹50,000 reward instead of ₹5000 as usual?'

'It's an error!' Asha squealed gleefully. 'Sshhh…!' Aarav looked around frantically. 'It's an error,' he confirmed in a quieter voice. 'When we were cataloguing the contents of the box Asha bought from the school shop, the coupon read ₹5000. Asha was adamant it was ₹50,000. And I said, it's always been ₹5000, so we went to Jahnvi James's house, where Asha first saw the ticket which Jahnvi had saved before her box was stolen. And sure enough…' Aarav pointed to the ticket on the table.

Asha pulled out another ticket, 'This one is from the one we bought at the school shop.'

Cash rewards of up to ₹5,000!

'And you think this is what the thief is after? A lottery coupon with an easy maths sum, and he could send in multiple entries?'

Karthik nodded, 'It's possible.' They all sat back thinking.

'I guess that means, the thief is just grabbing as many coupons as he can and plans to send multiple entries to the competition to win,' Karthik concluded.

'Except...' Asha raised a finger. You can't send in more than one entry. She pointed back to the rules and regulations, and Karthik read: *Only one entry per contestant*.

'So why steal more, then?' Karthik looked puzzled.

Aarav leaned forward, 'So what was your news?'

'Oh! I got the RFID kit.' Karthik's grin suddenly sank. 'But it's useless!'

'Why?'

'Because, if the thief is checking the contest tickets and stealing the boxes which offer ₹50,000 prize then he won't steal the one we have. What a waste!'

'Well...we might still be able to use it,' Asha began slowly.

'How?' Aarav retorted. 'We'd have to check everyone's boxes, and who is going to let us do that?'

'Yes,' Asha said with maddening calm. 'But what if we just swapped Jhanvi's ₹50,000 ticket for the original?'

CHAPTER 11

TECH TO THE RESCUE

The box was tagged, the coupon swapped and the bait left tantalisingly in a classroom that was used only sparingly for third languages.

Karthik had his RFID reader connected to the computer in their clubhouse, as the trio sat and waited.

'We'll get a beep when the box leaves the room. After that, we will need to carry the reader closer to track the box.'

'But what if it happens at night?' Asha asked. 'How will we know?'

'I'll get an alert on my phone and I'll message you immediately. Aarav and I will go if it's at night.'

'Agreed!' Aarav said firmly before Asha could raise arguments.

'Fine,' she responded sulkily. 'Meanwhile, let's talk about the printer.'

Aarav and Karthik groaned.

Aarav had spoken to the factory that manufactured Yuga geometry boxes again, to try to learn how the error came about. But it was a dead end, as the manufacturer got their coupon printing done elsewhere and the man on the other end of the line refused to say anything more.

'How on earth are we to search for the printer?' demanded Aarav.

'And even so, how could it matter?' added Karthik.

'I don't know, but that doesn't mean we shouldn't try and figure it out. We could...stake out the factory?'

'In Peenya? Even my mom would notice me gone for that long,' retorted Karthik.

Asha blinked at him, unperturbed. 'How would you go about it then?'

'I don't–' began Karthik.

'We could look on Google Maps for the printers in that area, and ask them?' ventured Aarav.

Karthik looked surprised. 'Sure, even if they don't do it themselves, they might know who?'

'Great, you look up Maps,' she pointed to Karthik, 'and you,' she added pointing to Aarav, 'make the calls.'

'And what are you doing?' Karthik and Aarav asked together as Asha made her way out of the clubhouse. 'I think I might have another idea about the printer...I'll let you know,' she added slamming the flap behind her.

Aarav and Karthik looked at each other.

'Yes, she's always like that,' Aarav answered before Karthik could say anything.

CHAPTER 12

ASHA STRIKES AGAIN

'V*a ma*...have you come alone?' Shop Uncle smiled gently at Asha as she entered the school bookshop for the second time that week. She smiled sweetly at him. 'No uncle. Mummy is waiting for anna to come... do you have chocolates?'

Shop Uncle laughed, and shook his head ruefully. 'No, I'm not allowed to sell chocolates. You can get them in the canteen. But don't eat too many! They aren't good for you.' He smiled benignly down at her.

Asha, who read about the exact working of the pancreas in regulating the amount of blood sugar (whose failure could lead to diabetes) did her best to maintain her sweetly blank expression. She let her eyes wander around the shop, and settle on the calendar behind the shopkeeper. 'What bird is that uncle?' she pointed.

‘It’s a bulbul, *kanna*. They are very small...like you! My son printed this calendar for me. He owns a printing press.’

‘Even Appa has a printer in office. Can he print this calendar?’ Asha tilted her head and goggled at the calendar. ‘Sure enough,’ Shop Uncle guffawed again.

For the case. For the case, Asha chanted mentally.

‘No ma...you need a biiiiig printer. He prints movie posters, ads and brochures, calendars. He works with big-big companies for all their printing needs. Every year he prints this calendar and gives it to all his customers as a gift. See?’ Shop Uncle lifted the calendar sheet to reveal another picture.

‘A pretty green bird on a pink tree?’ he described helpfully.

‘No uncle,’ Asha corrected, coldly dropping her act completely. ‘That’s a white-cheeked barbet sitting on a mimosa tree.’ Asha folded her arms and stared up at him imperiously.

‘Now where exactly is your son’s printing press located?’ she queried as he gaped at her.

CHAPTER 13

AN UN-GENIUS MOVE

Triumphantly, Asha re-entered the clubhouse...to find it empty.

Biting her lip, she sat down thinking hard. Could the boys have located the printer, too? Were they there already without her?

Asha looked around for the RFID reader. Grumpily, she realized that, once again, they had left her behind. But this time, she had an ace up her sleeve.

If she was right, then the RFID reader was probably leading the boys to the thief already. The only question was, how could she get there herself? Her parents wouldn't allow her to travel outside their apartment alone. And she couldn't possibly explain to the aunty at home about her sudden need to visit a printer.

She would have to bend the rules a bit. Again.

✧

'Do you hear that?' asked Karthik.

'I don't hear anything over this traffic.' replied Aarav grumpily.

They had reached the corner of Ulsoor and RK Mutt Road, with the RFID reader when the machine suddenly stopped beeping. The lane they had entered was a narrow one. Shops lined both sides, and the road was jam-packed with fruit vendors.

The boys had tried walking up and down the road in hopes of recapturing the signal. Neither wanted to admit defeat. But in truth, they had lost the signal.

'Scratchmidget!' cursed Karthik.

Aarav raised his eyebrows.

'What?'

'That's my word.'

'Yeah, so...have you patented it or something?' shot Karthik back.

'Is this really how you both have been spending your afternoon?' a voice floated along behind them.

The boys turned around to watch Asha gently rolling past them, as she sat pillion on the back seat of a cycle being pedalled by their ironing man.

'Asha!' the boys took off jogging after her.

'Where are you going? Anna! Stop!' Aarav panted after the cycle.

'It's right here at the end of the road, anna.' The cycle pulled over to the side of the building. Asha hopped off.

'Thank you, anna.'

'Ok *ma, anna koodu thirimbe po*.' He glared at Aarav and cycled away. Aarav goggled after him. The ironing man was generally friendly with everyone.

'What was that about?' gasped Karthik catching up.

'Oh, I just told him that Amma needed something from this shop, and Aarav hadn't returned yet. You know how distracted boys get...' she added grinning.

'Are-you-kidding-me!' Aarav managed to grind out. 'You're not allowed out of the apartment like this!'

'Not alone. That's why I asked Ironing Uncle,' Asha said blithely.

'That's exactly...that's not...you don't get...' Aarav spluttered into silence and turned to Karthik for support.

'That was incredibly stupid of you.'

Gaping, Asha rounded on him. Aarav took a protective step back. Before she could respond Karthik added, 'There are strangers, and there are acquaintances and there are friends and there is family. AND...' he said loudly over her protests, 'there's a reason why your parents said to go with Aarav only. And if you aren't smart enough to understand why...talk to your mom again and ask.'

Abruptly Asha closed her mouth. The trio stared at each other.

In the silence, Aarav cleared his throat. 'Why are you here, Asha?'

Fixing Karthik with one last glare, Asha pointed carelessly over her shoulder. 'That's the printer's address.'

Asha took a deep breath, and narrated her suspicions about Shop Uncle's printer son. 'But I wasn't able to confirm if he's the printer who does the contest chits for the geometry box.' She muttered something else after that.

'What?'

Asha glared. 'I said, Shop Uncle got furious and chased me out. You'll probably need to manage all my school supply purchases for the next few years or so,' she added sulkily.

Karthik grinned and Aarav tried his best not to laugh. 'You blew your cover?'

'Blew your top, more like it,' added Aarav giving in to laughter.

'Alright. Fine!' Asha held up a hand. 'I could have kept my cover and found out...but the point is, I got here first.'

'Hey we almost had it, too,' Karthik retorted waving the RFID scanner.

Aarav held up his hands to short-circuit the feud, 'Well, either way, we have all reached the place. Shall we go up and confront him?'

CHAPTER 14

GOING...NOWHERE

Unsure of what to expect, Aarav led the way up a narrow flight of stairs. A flickering tubelight barely illuminated the landing on the first floor, which housed a tailoring shop. Silently, Asha pointed him further up the staircase.

Nervously, the trio climbed one flight further up.

At the top of the stairs was a poorly painted signboard that stated MURUGESH'S PRINTING PRESS was this way, with a wobbly arrow, helpfully pointing them in the right direction.

'You'd think a printer would print his own signboard,' muttered Aarav. He was hastily shushed by the other two. They stood outside the door of the printing press. Should they knock? Should they barge in? They looked at each other, uncertainly.

Karthik moved forward and pushed open the door. 'Follow my lead,' he muttered. Behind him, Aarav rolled his eyes.

Inside, the noise was unbelievable. A loud racketing that was muted from outside was making the most of it closest to the door. Cheap flyers which Aarav often found in the dozens with the morning newspaper were strewn everywhere.

Further in, were larger electronic printers that were churning out glossy, unfolded brochures with a quiet humming whine, as lights flashed back and forth.

Packages wrapped in brown paper were stacked like bricks around the room. Through these, the kids could make out an enclosed glass cabin at the end of the hall, where a man sat working. Karthik was already leading them toward him.

Warily, Aarav looked around. During their last adventure, the boys had been trapped in a place much like this. There only seemed to be one person in the printing office, but that didn't mean others wouldn't come. Making a quick decision, Aarav stopped in his tracks and whispered to Asha, 'You go ahead, I'll guard the exit, and make sure we aren't trapped here.' She turned and nodded seriously, giving him a silent thumbs up.

Feeling both scared and very grown up, Aarav stationed himself between the piles of printed material, where he could watch the door without being seen. Beside him were some of the calendars that Asha had described from the bookshop, in addition to many others.

If the RFID tracker led them here, could the missing geometry boxes be lying around somewhere? Quietly, he began to snoop.

✧

Karthik, now within view of the man in the office, strode up to the door and opened it. 'Sir, are you Mr Palani's son?'

Asha mentally replaced Shop Uncle's name with Mr Palani.

To her eyes, the man in the glass cabin looked like a bent pin. Tall, skinny, with a big head, Murugesh stooped over his table, though his clothes were clean and neatly ironed. *Neat as a pin, too,* Asha smiled sweetly at him.

Murugesh's irritation at being disturbed softened when he heard his dad's name. 'That's me. Did Appa send you?'

'Yes, we're from the school,' Karthik entered all the way in and looked surprised for a moment at Aarav's absence.

Asha covered the moment up, 'Shop Uncle said you could help us with printing a poster for our school?'

Murugesh nodded. 'Of course! You have the design?'

'Errr...' Karthik and Asha exchanged glances. Murugesh laughed. 'I need either the text that you want on the poster or the final design. Do you know what size you need?'

'A3,' replied Asha confidently, having heard this discussion involving posters for her mother's bakery.

Smaller numbers meant bigger sizes, and bigger numbers like A5 meant smaller sheets. Grown-ups were rarely logical, but in this case, Asha had read that it was actually a mathematical proportion that gave each sheet its number.

'OK, how many copies?'

'Fifty.'

'When do you need it?'

'By the 15th.'

The conversation seemed to be getting rapidly out of their control. And where was Aarav? Karthik wondered how to bring the conversation gently back to their investigation, when Asha said, 'Do you do the coupon printing for Yuga geometry boxes?'

So much for being gentle.

Murugesh's friendly expression froze. 'Who told you that?'

'The Peenya Factory.' Asha had completely taken over the interrogation now, as Karthik stood helplessly beside her. 'I noticed the contest ticket showed the wrong value, and I called them to ask if I could still send in my entry. They said I could exchange the ticket here?' she added innocently.

Murugesh relaxed. 'Oh, yes...no problem.' He opened his drawer, took out a set of keys and walked towards a greenish-grey steel bureau behind him. Unlocking it, he pulled out a sheaf of tickets wrapped in a rubber band. 'Just one, right?'

'Five, actually,' answered Karthik before Asha could.

Murugesh laughed. 'You know you can only send one entry, right?'

'Yes, but some of my friends lost theirs when their geometry boxes were stolen.' Karthik improvised. Murugesh's expression closed again, as he silently counted out five tickets and handed them to him. 'I'll need to note your name, and class. Your friends' too,' Karthik gave it to him, wildly mixing up the first and last names of his classmates and changing the sections.

'So um...we will bring our design tomorrow?' Karthik added as they began to head out the door.

'Sure. You can come directly after school. Or you can even send it through my brother. He's in 9B.'

'Ayyapan right?' added Asha smugly.

Murugesh looked surprised. 'You know him?'

'Shop Uncle told me.'

Murugesh smiled again and led them out through the crush of paper material. Aarav was still nowhere to be seen. Racking his brain, Karthik tried to think of anything else he could ask to delay leaving. But before he could open his mouth, Murugesh herded them out the main door. 'Sorry, lots of work. I'll see you tomorrow, OK?'

And he shut the door.

Asha and Karthik stood on the landing and heard the lock bolt slide in.

The landing and stairwell were empty.

That meant Aarav was still inside.

CHAPTER 15

THE WAITING

Downstairs, tucked away in a small, dirty gully off the main road, Asha and Karthik continued to whisper in soft voices. The evening light was almost gone, and there was still no sign of Aarav.

'We just have to wait till Murugesh leaves, and then we can get him out. He's probably waiting for the same thing.'

Eyes round behind her thick glasses, Asha nodded.

It had been a good idea to keep a watch, but they hadn't the faintest idea what had happened to Aarav who should have been close to the door. Deep down, Karthik was worried. *What if Aarav was in trouble?*

'He wouldn't have left the shop without us.' He added comfortingly.

They both felt restless standing there and waiting. The mosquitoes didn't help either.

And Karthik was doing his best to keep Asha from going to the printing press, hammering on the door and blowing their story.

After they had agreed to wait, Asha remained disturbingly silent. It was starting to get dark, and Asha and Aarav's parents would be home soon.

Karthik smacked at his arm.

'What's that whine?' whispered Asha.

'The mosquit–' abruptly, Karthik shut his mouth. They both looked at his backpack. The RFID reader was beeping again.

✧

Well this is great, thought Aarav as he tried his best to get more comfortable. Brown packages of stacked paper not only looked like bricks, but felt like them, too. He had been on the wrong side of the stacks, with no way to exit when he heard the group leaving. By moving a few packages around, Aarav tucked himself deeper into the stacks, and out of sight from anyone walking by. But it certainly wasn't comfortable.

Now after waiting for nearly an hour, he was beginning to get worried. What if Murugesh didn't leave? What if he had to use the bathroom? No sooner did that thought occur to him, than he began to fidget more. *Great work,*

Aarav. Had to act like the smart one, trying to think ahead, and now see what happened.

Not only had Aarav not found any stolen geometry boxes, he hadn't heard the conversation the two had with Murugesh. Aarav continued to berate himself silently when he heard a sharp knock on the door. He held his breath. Was it Karthik or Asha who was back to find him? He stealthily readied himself to escape as soon as the door opened.

Still hidden between the stacks, Aarav watched Murugesh's polished shoes stride by. Breathing slowly, he tried to calm his racing heart.

'*Nee-ah*? What happened?'

'I got one more, anna,' a young voice replied.

'Come inside.'

Murugesh and a boy (wearing the same uniform from Aarav's school), walked back into the cabin.

Waiting till they settled inside, Aarav began to crawl his way towards the door. Carefully he reached up to the door, peering back to ensure he couldn't be seen...and froze.

The young boy was holding out a geometry box to Murugesh.

'Scratchmidget!' breathed Aarav.

Should he stay and listen or escape to safety? His legs were pleading with him to get out the door, but Aarav resisted. He couldn't let their AKA club down. This was why they were here! And just maybe he could solve the case.

He slowly slid back down and was about to crawl back towards the cabin, when the door opened and hit him in the bum. Startled, he whirled around and came nose-to-nose with Karthik, who was also crawling his way in.

Silently, with a variety of expressions he had never seen on Karthik's face before, Aarav gathered that Karthik was relieved to see him, mad that he had disappeared on them, and excited by the very same thing.

The stolen geometry box!

Nodding, Aarav gave him the thumbs up and pointed towards the cabin. Looking back, he motioned firmly for Asha to stay outside the door.

Asha stuck her tongue at him, and continued to crawl in behind Karthik.

Rolling his eyes, Aarav turned around and together they crept towards the cabin, where Murugesh and the boy were arguing.

CHAPTER 16

NOT AN ACCIDENT

'I don't want to keep doing this,' the boy was saying.

'Do we have a choice?' answered Murugesh in a harsher voice than they had heard earlier.

There was a sharp clanking noise, as though the metal box was being hammered opened. But from their low position, no one could make out what was happening.

'It's not here.' The distinct sound of a metal box being thrown to the floor, followed.

'We are never going to find anything. Let's just tell him,' pleaded the younger boy.

'No.'

'Anna, pl–'

'We have no choice. If it comes out, we will lose everything. My printing business. And you, too. You'll be expelled. And what do you think will happen to appa? All of it will be gone in this one mistake.'

'But it was just an accid–'

'Don't be a child. You and I know it was no accident. Clean that up. I'm almost done here and we can go home together.'

Frantically, Asha signalled the boys and together they rapidly crawled their way to the door. Opening it noiselessly, one by one they slipped out.

✧

It was late next morning, when Karthik and Aarav met in their clubhouse.

The weekend had just begun. And with an amazing combination of timing and luck, Asha and Aarav's parents were unaware of their late adventure the previous evening. They were, however, well aware that Asha had made an excursion out of the apartment. The ironing man had reported it to his wife, who in turn told an apartment maid, who told their neighbour, who (of course) told Asha's mother. Asha was grounded for the weekend.

'And I'm supposed to record our meetings for her, or else,' groaned Aarav bringing Karthik up to speed on their home situation as he pulled out their old backup mobile phone and pressed the recording app.

Karthik nodded seriously.

'Saturday, 22 September, 9.47 a.m.' saying this, Karthik let out a long sigh and leaned back in his chair. The trio had raced home yesterday and had very little time to discuss what they had heard. Various versions of 'what on earth was that all about' pretty much summed it up.

'Let's start by recording what we know,' suggested Aarav who was thinking along the same lines.

Karthik nodded again.

'That boy,' Aarav began.

'Ayyapan, Murugesh's brother and Mr Palani's son.' Karthik supplied.

Startled, Aarav sat back.

'We knew Murugesh was being a bit weird yesterday when we talked about the stolen geometry boxes,' Karthik continued. 'But he didn't seem to mind admitting that he printed Yuga contest tickets or that there was an error in the printing. Look he gave us new ones,' Karthik pulled out five tightly rolled tickets from his pocket and dropped them on the table.

Aarav examined the tickets carefully. 'These look fine to me…just no printing error. ₹5000 reward.'

'Yeah,' agreed Karthik. 'But his brother is stealing them, and Murugesh knows why.'

'What were they hammering the box open for? Could you see?'

'No. Asha?'

'No, she didn't either. Though she had some theories on alloyed metals.'

Laughing, Karthik shook his head. 'Let's remember what they said. Ayyapan didn't want to steal boxes anymore–'

'And Murugesh said, they had no choice.'

'And Ayyapan said, they wouldn't find anything and to tell...him? Them?'

'Him, definitely. And that it was an accident.'

'To which Murugesh said, it was no accident, and that they would lose everything.'

Silently, the boys once again recapped the conversation in their heads. It was obvious to the trio that they had found their geometry box thief. But they were no closer to knowing why the boxes were being stolen.

Everyone in the school (except Asha most recently) liked Shop Uncle. What would happen to him, if it came out one son was stealing boxes and the other son had something to do with it?

'Do you think the printing error wasn't an accident?' ventured Aarav.

'Well if it wasn't an accident, then maybe Murugesh has to get those coupons back or lose his job, printing for Yuga?'

'But that doesn't make any sense.'

Replaying the events in his head for the millionth time, Karthik tried to recollect Murugesh's exact expression. 'Murugesh had been worried when Asha said she knew he did the coupon printing. But when she mentioned the Peenya factory, he just handed us the tickets. Great on-the-spot bluffing, by the way, Asha.' Karthik added to the recording phone.

'So now what?'

Gloomily, Karthik sank back in his chair.

'I have absolutely no idea.'

CHAPTER 17

AARAV THINKS FAST

It was a gloomy, wet-weather Bengaluru morning. Rather than meet in the crowded canteen where most students were avoiding the light drizzle, the trio huddled under one of the large Flame of the Forest trees, which kept the ground below relatively dry.

Morosely, they had continued to discuss theories and plans all week, without any agreement. Asha, unsurprisingly, was all for going straight to the principal. Until Karthik pointed out that they had no proof. Not even a broken geometry box.

Aarav thought about using the RFID tag again, but what was the point? They already knew who the thief was. They even knew where the stolen geometry boxes were going. The big question was *why*.

'Something is inside those geometry boxes,' stated

Karthik categorically. 'Otherwise, why are they going through so much trouble?'

'OK, let's just pretend that "something" is small and well hidden,' responded Asha. 'Like a microchip?'

'I doubt they'd be hammering away if it was a microchip,' muttered Aarav.

'Hence, I said *pretend*,' ground out Asha.

It had been like this all weekend. Tempers frayed as they discussed various options as to what could be hidden. And the even more tantalising question...how was this *not* an accident?

'Whatever it is,' cut in Karthik, 'has to be from the Peenya factory. Who else could insert something into the metal case itself? Murugesh only does the coupon printing. He delivers it, and the assembly happens at the factory, right?'

'But then how is Murugesh involved at all? Or his brother?'

Karthik shrugged. 'Maybe someone at Peenya told him to collect it, and he lost it?'

'Drugs?' breathed Aarav. Grimly, Karthik looked at him.

'What if it is?'

'And Ayyapan saw it or took it by accident?'

'Or misdelivered it,' added Asha.

'And they have to refund or replace it, so they are searching.'

Aarav chewed on his lip. 'It kind of fits. But we don't yet have all the answers.'

Just then the first bell rang. Their break would be over in five minutes. 'The key is Ayyapan. We need to follow him.' Asha began re-packing her bag.

'He's in 9th,' Aarav protested. 'How are we going to do that?'

'Do you know anyone in his class, who might be able to watch him for us?' asked Asha.

Silently both boys shook their heads. 'And I'd rather not let everyone know we are on to him, until we know what it's really about,' Karthik added.

'Stealing is stealing,' Asha stated unperturbed.

'Yeah…but what if he's being blackmailed or something?' Karthik also picked up his backpack.

'Oh come on…he's in 9th standard!'

'I agree, let's not alert anyone until we know–' Aarav abruptly turned and stared across the field. It was Ayyapan, and he was making his way into the room where their school's sports equipment was shopd.

Rapidly, Aarav slung his backpack over his shoulder.

'Asha, I'll see you after school.' To Karthik, he said 'Let's meet at the clubhouse, later,' and dashed through the drizzle. Keeping an eye out for any teacher, Aarav reached the door of the sports room and peeked inside.

'Don't you mess with me boy, I'll– Hey! Who are you, man?' Round, loud, and with a short fuse, Nagesh Sir, was the senior school PT teacher. Unpopularly known as 'Nuggets', his greasy finger (which had been rummaging around in a fast-food paper carton), was now pointing at Aarav.

Stepping forward, Aarav said the first wild thing that came into his head. 'Sir, Principal Sir is calling you.' Gulping, he watched in amazement as Nuggets jumped up, and waddled around his desk, wiping his fingers on his shirt. He grabbed a battered baseball cap and covered his balding head and headed towards the door. 'Wait here.' He barked over his shoulder at the frozen Ayyapan.

'YOU! Go to class, man!' Nuggets roared at Aarav gesturing him out, before shouldering his way behind him.

Aarav had no choice but to leave.

CHAPTER 18

IT'S STILL OUT THERE

'Nuggets, man...that took guts.' Karthik shook his head admiringly after Aarav finished narrating his very brief encounter in the school shoproom.

'It could just be a coincidence,' Asha, having never encountered the rage of Nuggets on the field, was far less impressed.

'Asha, you didn't hear him...he said don't mess with me...I'm sure he's involved. He's probably the one Ayyapan was referring to.'

'Then why would he ask Murugesh to tell him?' countered Asha. 'Ayyapan is obviously talking directly to Chicken Nuggets.'

Guffawing, Karthik nodded. 'That does seem logical. And Nuggets is always threatening someone or the other. If it was Nuggets who has lost, or wants something from the box, Murugesh wouldn't be involved right?'

Aarav shook his head furiously. 'You're just guessing. Both of you! I know what I heard!' Huffing, Aarav dropped himself into a beanbag.

'OK fine. Let's assume Nuggets is involved. We are still no closer to getting an answer to what or why.'

'But...neither are they!' To the boys utter amazement, Asha began drumming her fists on the table in excitement.

Jumping up, she rolled her eyes at their continued puzzlement. '*They* haven't found it yet. That means whatever it is, is still out there! We just need to find it first.'

'Are you proposing that we start stealing geometry boxes, too?' asked Karthik bemusedly.

'No! Just borrowing and inspecting. Look!' Asha waved at their computer. 'We have the list of people who have had their boxes stolen.'

'Yeah, so?'

'But when Aarav and I went around, there were some kids who still had their geometry boxes right? Who *didn't* have them stolen. They kept them extra carefully. And now with everyone hyper alert, Ayyapan can't get to them, easily. He only got ours, because we left it as a bait!' Asha was now positively vibrating with excitement.

'But he hasn't found what he is looking for,' said Aarav slowly.

'And we can!' Gasping, the trio found themselves on their feet.

Aarav suddenly sobered up, as he remembered their last door-to-door excursion. 'That's a lot of boxes to go through.'

'Ugh.' Deflated Asha sat back down. 'How about we just check those who have the wrong ticket?'

'Of course…' breathed Karthik. The siblings turned to him in unison. 'It's an identifier! For that particular batch! Murugesh must have done it intentionally. So, if you have the wrong ticket, bring it to him and get the right one. He noted our names! And Ayyapan can come to find you and check or steal your box.'

'So we just need to find out who has not had their box stolen, *and* has the misprinted ticket.' concluded Asha.

'Before Ayyapan.' added Karthik

'And without Nuggets, or Murugesh and anyone at school getting suspicious,' finished Aarav.

'OK,' Karthik leaned forward. The siblings leaned in as well.

'We need a game plan.'

CHAPTER 19

SKILL LEVEL: 1, TIME: NIL

Aarav sighed sullenly, as he rang the next doorbell.

Karthik's game plan was remarkably simple. Asha ran through their Excel sheet, and added the names of those whom she recalled still having their Yuga geometry boxes. Impressively, she remembered at least sixteen names. So that's where they decided Aarav would start.

To avoid angry aunties, and uncooperative scratchmidgets, Aarav carried a box of his mother's decorative cookies, which he sweetly offered if a parent opened the door, along with a flyer of his mom's bakery. His mom had been requesting this for over a year now and was delighted to supply both the cookies and the flyers. *Brownie points*, thought Aarav with a smirk.

And if a kid opened the door, a swift negotiation of cookies ensued, for the privilege of being allowed to inspect their geometry box. If the coupon showed the wrong award, Aarav would then hand the box to Asha who would quickly conduct a forensic examination, with Karthik at her side making notes.

They obviously couldn't destroy the boxes. So, using a delicate hammer, Asha learned what the 'right' sound was when she tapped on the metal box. Anything thicker or hidden in the metal container would sound different, and if that happened, they would either buy the box outright, or try and swap the box with another one. So far, Asha, who had driven Aarav nearly insane by tapping the spare Yuga boxes they had bought all night long; hadn't indicated that there was anything unusual with the boxes they were checking.

Now that Aarav had finished knocking on around ten doors, he was beginning to wonder if they were barking up the wrong tree.

Karthik and Asha said it was merely the maths. Karthik (who, amongst the teachers, was also known as Mr Perfect Score for maths brilliance in school) said that their odds of finding it went up with every box they checked. It had a lot to do with probability and statistics, but as the only non-maths head in the trio, Aarav tuned out early and decided to take their word for it.

Secretly, Aarav was very worried.

Word of their questions would undoubtedly circle through the school, soon enough. Ayyapan would definitely hear about it. And Murugesh also knew their names and faces, and only had to connect the two. To top it all off, Aarav had outright *lied* to Nuggets about the principal, and so was probably on his radar, too. Though there was a small chance he would not be recognized by the strict PT master who routinely mixed up all their names.

Whichever way you looked at it, they were running short of time.

Heaving another sigh, Aarav rang the next doorbell.

✧

Glumly, the trio dragged their feet back to their clubhouse. The evening had turned dark quickly and the overcast weather reflected their moods aptly.

Fourteen Yuga boxes had been inspected (two more had been stolen since they last checked), but none of them had turned up with anything secreted in the box.

Karthik dropped the test pad, on which he had been making notes down on their battered table, and turned on their computer to update their Excel sheet.

'Now what?' asked Aarav grumpily as he pulled out some drinks and snacks and handed them around.

'Back to the drawing board, of course,' Asha muttered. Aarav, seeing her lips mouth the word 'loser', flared up in anger.

'Forget it! I'm not going door to door again. I'm done.'

'Calm down,' Karthik turned towards them.

'You calm down! I'm the one who has to always do all the talking and it's just not fair.'

'That's your strength, Aarav. Why wouldn't we use it?'

Stumped into silence by what seemed like a compliment, Aarav stared.

Karthik moved back towards the desk. 'You have the skills to talk to multiple people. I don't.' He waved a hand to Asha. 'Sometimes Asha can do it, too, but this is your biggest skill. Asha is a walking encyclopaedia, and that helps us connect the dots.'

He leaned back in his chair, and gazed at the top of their tank. 'I do the maths. I can build stuff. We each have skills which make this team strong.'

Karthik looked to both the brooding siblings. 'We can't quit now. We've made a lot of progress in this case. Dude, we've already found out who's been doing the stealing, which is more than what three school principals could do!'

Asha nodded. 'Let's just take a break for the rest of the day.'

She looked at Aarav.

'We can't,' he responded bleakly. Quickly he filled them in on his fears. 'It's only a matter of a day, when the news runs through school again. Ayyapan or Nuggets is going to come after us.'

The group stared at each other in silence.

'Fine.' Asha stood up, though her short height made very little difference to the dramatic effect she was going for. Karthik hid a smile. 'But let's split it up.' She turned towards Karthik. 'Aarav is right, he can't do all the talking and this is going too slow already. You and I have heard how he approaches each house over a dozen times now. We will just imitate what he says and see how it goes.'

Karthik nodded nervously. He was the most disliked among all the apartment kids. 'I guess it's time to up our skills. We'll split the blocks up, and finish this tonight.' He looked at Asha.

'Do you have any spare hammers?'

CHAPTER 20

SLEDGEHAMMERED

It was gruelling work, Karthik could admit. He had to give Aarav more credit for sticking it out so long. It was nerve-wracking to ring a stranger's bell, and not know what kind of reaction you were going to get. Sometimes friendly, sometimes cold. And in Karthik's case, three times hostile. He noted those doors down on his sheet for Aarav to work his magic later. Then dragged his courage back up to go and ring the next door.

Unfortunately, the next door was one of those long musical sing-songy chimes which Karthik particularly hated. As he waited for the chime to end (so he could ring again) the door opened.

A burly boy, whom Karthik recognized as a 9th standard kid from his school, filled the door frame. Karthik took a step back.

'Oh, it's you. What do you want?'

'Hi! Let's Loaf Bakery in Indiranagar is offering these free cookie samples...' Karthik reeled off the standard dialogue, while his heart pounded. He handed over a leaflet. The boy took both and was about to close the door, when Karthik extended a hand to stop him.

'Hey, I was just wondering if...'

'You don't need to see my geometry box.'

'W-what?'

'I said, you don't need to see my geometry box. It's a

Yuga brand, it hasn't been stolen.'

'I could give you another box of–'

'No.'

Karthik had already met some of the hostile kids. But this was different. Puzzled, he said, 'How did you know that's what I was here for?'

The burly boy folded his arms. 'Ayyapan is my friend.'

'So?' countered Karthik, his mind racing furiously.

'Soooo...you are trying to make trouble for him.'

'Why would seeing your geometry box make trouble for your friend?' asked Karthik trying to channel Asha's innocent tone.

Eyes narrowed, the burly boy leaned forward. Karthik, half a foot shorter leaned back.

'You are not going to solve this case. And you are going to leave my friend alone. He's only trying to protect his family.' Contemptuously, the boy leaned back against the door of his frame and looked Karthik up and down. 'And what would you know of that?'

The boy's eyes glittered with malice as he continued. 'Besides, I understand a boy like you could afford to pay the price. Maybe you are already.'

'What?' Karthik was truly confused now.

'Maybe that's the source of your perfect score.'

'What?'

'You wouldn't want to be on the wrong side of Nuggets, either. Drop this stupid investigation. And leave my friend alone.'

The door slammed shut in Karthik's face. He stared at the closed door a moment longer.

'What?'

CHAPTER 21

A STEP BACK

It was nearly midnight, by the time the trio had finished their survey, had dinner and snuck up to their clubhouse as agreed upon.

With cold determination, Karthik had finished his list, his encounter with Ayyapan's friend leaving him less afraid of all the other houses.

The hardest part was facing exactly the words that had been hurled at him. Rich enough to pay the price for...something. Wouldn't know anything about saving his family. *No guesses needed there. And the source of his perfect score? What the hell was that about?* Karthik knew the other kids resented him for all that he had, and mocked him for what he didn't have, a complete family.

It hurt. But after having it thrown into his face, it unexpectedly...hurt less.

The rest of the houses yielded results, but they still hadn't found a box hiding anything. Neither of the siblings had been successful either.

Pushing his feelings aside, Karthik quickly cut to the chase. 'That kid knew Ayyapan had been stealing the boxes. He knows why and he knows what, and he knows what Nuggets's involvement is.'

'I told you Nuggets was involved,' yawned Aarav.

'And Murugesh, too, if that's what the family comment meant,' added Asha.

Karthik nodded. 'I feel we have all the pieces, but...'

'Look, the worst has happened,' said Aarav oddly echoing Karthik's thoughts. 'We've run through all the houses and found nothing in the boxes. And Ayyapan is already on to us, or that boy wouldn't have said those things to you.'

Karthik and Asha nodded.

'I think the best we can do is take all this to the principal tomorrow and let him handle it,' Aarav concluded.

Karthik rubbed his face blearily. It had been a very long day. 'Not the principal, we still have no proof. Let's take it to Daniel Sir.' Daniel Sir was their middle school Maths teacher, which meant he knew the 9th standard boys, too. He was very popular with the kids due to his wry sense of humour. Plus he always took students' questions and concerns seriously.

'If he believes us, he'll know how to tackle Nuggets.'

Asha sighed. 'But we are so close.' She put her chin down on the table. 'It feels like we are quitting.'

Aarav put a hand on her shoulder. 'It does, but I don't think we can go any further. We've run out of places to look for geometry boxes. And we are dangerously close to accusing a teacher of something, and we don't even know what!'

'It's time to take a step back.'

CHAPTER 22

A STEP FORWARD

Early the next morning, Asha and Aarav's mother was having a bad start to her day. The kids had overslept and were running late. Bags that were supposed to be packed the previous night had not been done and so there was the usual manic scramble for books.

'I just don't know how many times to tell you both,' fumed their mother slamming Aarav's tiffin box on the table. Aarav hastily stuffed it into his bag as he continued wolfing down his breakfast. Today's was an egg dosa with spicy coconut chutney, and some grilled veggies on the side.

'And where are your answer papers, Aarav? You were supposed to get them signed, right?'

Choking, Aarav stuffed the last bite into his mouth and ran to find his answer papers. Amid their investigation, he had completely forgotten. The term was coming to an end and he had to show his signed answer papers to the class teacher to get his report card. They had already been reminded in class and today was the last day.

'I've already got mine signed,' Asha added with maddening calm. She continued to chew her dosa at a measured pace.

'Asha, come on, we're going to be late!' Aarav tossed over his shoulder as he zoomed past her to his room, to gather up his answer papers. Maths, physics, biology (he grimaced at his marks), history...what else? English, language, where was his chemistry paper?

He dug into his drawer and then into his bag. And then into his closet. The answer paper was nowhere to be seen. 'Ahhh...scratchmidget!' Aarav cursed and ran back to his mother who was silently glowering now. Asha was already at the door.

Rapidly, she signed the papers, propelled them all out of the door and left. Aarav didn't bother with his cycle, as he and his sister took off running. They lived less than a few hundred metres from their school, and could still make it before the gates shut.

'I lost my chemistry answer sheet, Asha is...it...with... you...?' he huffed at her, rubbing at a stitch in his side.

'Why would I have your answer paper?' retorted Asha.

'Just check once, *na*!' pleaded Aarav as they entered the gates and were about to part ways to their respective blocks.

Grudgingly, Asha opened her bag wide, and stepped back as Aarav practically dived into it. Asha, as always, was meticulously neat. Her textbooks were stacked separately from her notebooks, and she had used her test pad as a bag divider.

'Where are your papers?' Aarav panted.

Silently she pointed to the jute folder next to the test pad. Rapidly (as the second bell rang for assembly), he

looked through her papers. His chemistry sheet wasn't mixed up with her papers. It was easy to see, as Asha had neatly stapled each question paper to her answer sheet.

Rolling his eyes, he handed them back. 'Who keeps their question papers like this?'

'I do, obviously. I file every–' but Aarav had already trotted off, shoving her papers into her hands and leaving her bag half open.

Sighing, she rearranged her books to her liking and calmly continued, carrying her papers to the class. She didn't hurry. What most kids (her idiot brother included) didn't realize was that being studious and well-known for following all the rules, gave her chances to bend the rules once in a while. Teachers would see her out of class, but never ask why. Because a girl like Asha never cut class. She was a topper. And class leader. Obviously, she must be doing something responsible.

Unlike her brother, Asha would have been able to easily explain to her teacher if any of her papers had gone missing. She'd just say something like...someone's mother had borrowed her answer paper to teach her son, and hadn't returned it yet. Easy. Believable. And most importantly, not her fault. These were the benefits of being a class topper.

Asha paused in mid-step.

Class topper. Mr Perfect Score.

Asha tapped her papers on her head thinking hard.

'Oh god...of course! Of course!' Asha turned on her heel and raced back towards the middle school block.

CHAPTER 23

ASHA'S EPIPHANY

'Asha, have you lost your mind?' whispered Aarav.

She had raced back and caught him just before he joined his class line for assembly. Dragging him to the narrow gap behind the stage, she ran away again and came back tugging a bemused-looking Karthik behind her.

'Do you know what this place is?' hissed Aarav.

Karthik gave him a pointed look. Admittedly, Aarav hadn't wanted to explain to his sister how there were some private nooks around the school that you didn't go to. Unless you were seniors looking to avoid the eyes of teachers and...even thinking about it made him uncomfortable. Aarav swatted the thought from his head and focused on what Asha was saying.

'I know what it is! I know what they are looking for!' she did a little jig for them. In the background, the school song was over and the mike was being adjusted with its usual cacophony of screeches.

'Well, spit it out, we're already going to be in trouble for being late,' Aarav said sourly.

'*Vandalism is a disgusting habit! We will not tolerate it in this school!*' the principal was back to booming his usual morning pleasantries.

'And it ties up perfectly with everything,' continued Asha, hugging herself.

'Asha...' growled Karthik warningly. Asha merely smiled impishly back.

'And if I catch one more student scraping their name into the desks or writing profanity on the bathroom walls, they will be expelled! No second chances.'

'I'll give you a hint,' grinned Asha.

'This is no time for games, Asha, we are supposed to talk to Daniel Sir today, remember?'

Asha looked at both the boys, glaring down at her uniformly. She sighed.

'It's simple.' She turned to Karthik. 'Toppers can get off lightly when they get caught breaking rules, right?'

'Right,' confirmed Karthik, much to Aarav's astonishment.

Unable to contain her excitement, Asha did a little twirl as she continued to explain, 'But how does an average student, suddenly become a topper?'

'*...and they will be treated the same way we deal with anyone caught stealing or cheating! Immediate expulsion. No second chances!*' the principal's voice washed on over them.

Asha's smile turned wicked, as the boys continued to gaze at her blankly.

'Still don't get it? Losers! He cheated. Ayyapan cheated.'

'OK, so?' Aarav continued to look blank, as Karthik sucked his breath in.

Karthik turned to Aarav. 'He didn't just copy cheat, he cheated because he got the question paper.'

'And who does the printing for all our school question papers?' added Asha innocently, tilting her head.

'Murugesh!' The boys responded back.

'Of course! It makes perfect sense.' Karthik paced their limited space, while thinking out loud. 'Murugesh printed the question papers, and Ayyapan somehow got access, and he secreted the question paper into a geometry box. And then what? Lost it?' he turned back to Asha, who shrugged.

'But what about, "Just tell him it was an accident"?' added Aarav. 'Who is "him"?'

'Nuggets.' Karthik and Asha responded.

'But what does Nuggets have to do with it?' exclaimed Aarav.

'My question is, what business is it of yours?'

Frozen in shock, the trio turned. In their elation, they hadn't realized the assembly had ended.

And Nuggets was standing right behind them.

CHAPTER 24

NUGGETS IS...CHICKEN

'So three big detectives are trying to get me fired, eh?'

'Sir…no sir, we were just…'

'Don't think I don't know what you have been up to. After that trick with the principal, I told that boy to keep an eye on you. Asking questions about geometry boxes. *Periyyaa-CBI officers! Thoo!*'

Nuggets had brought them back to his tiny office off the side of the school shoproom and was pacing around in a towering temper.

'I've been here for decades, you hear me? Decades! It's my word against yours.'

'Sir,' cautiously, Karthik raised his hands, 'we've already talked to Daniel Sir.'

'WHAT?' roared Nuggets.

Karthik kept talking, 'You've been leaking the exam papers to kids with money. And when Ayyapan approached you for his exams, you started blackmailing him and his brother to help print and distribute them.'

'USELESS BUGGERS!' Nuggets threw a helmet across the room where it smashed into a glass cabinet of dusty trophies.

The trio leaped back in shock. Aarav moved Asha behind him.

Before they could say another word, Nuggets grabbed his keys and his much-abused baseball hat, threw open the door to his office with a bang and left.

'G-good bluffing, Karthik,' panted Asha. Quickly, they left out of the room, and walked rapidly down the corridor. Gulping, Karthik shook his head. 'I wasn't bluffing.'

'How did you figure it out?' gasped Aarav. 'That Nuggets was blackmailing them?'

'Murugesh said it was no accident. Ayyapan had started the problem by cheating first. And it looks like Nuggets tried to take advantage of Ayyapan and his brother, but something went wrong.'

Together, the trio headed towards the administrative buildings, as Karthik continued.

'I think Ayyapan was stealing to recover the question papers they had hidden in the boxes.'

'Remember, what that boy said? Back at the apartment?'

They stopped outside of the principal's office. Karthik looked from one sibling to the other.

'Ayyapan was trying to protect his family.'

CHAPTER 25

BUT WHERE'S THE PROOF?

Half the school day was over, and they still hadn't attended a single class. The principal had listened to them carefully, then called in the vice principal and junior school headmistress, and made them tell the story all over again. He then told them to sit in the waiting room and not discuss this further with anyone.

Two hours later, they were called back in.

'So you are saying, that Ayyapan would take the question paper from Nagesh, make copies at his brother's shop, slip them into geometry boxes, and sell them directly to students while helping his father in the shop?'

Asha nodded. 'But this time, his father sold the boxes before Ayyapan could.'

'And they have been afraid of some student coming forward and the entire operation coming to light,' concluded the principal gravely.

'So Nagesh made Ayyapan steal the boxes back,' added Aarav. It seemed important to stress that Ayyapan was a reluctant thief.

The principal steepled his fingers together. 'But here is the problem. Without actually having any evidence, I cannot accuse Murugesh or Ayyapan, or Nagesh of misconduct. In fact, Mr Nagesh is no longer reachable, either on phone or at home.'

'Wouldn't Murugesh be able to confirm?' asked Aarav curiously.

The principal raised his eyebrows. 'And why would he admit it? It would implicate him and his brother, too, wouldn't it? Plus no one in this school has come forward saying they found a leaked question paper in their geometry box,' he added wryly. 'So where is the proof?'

'Besides,' he continued gently, 'Ayyapan's father has already obtained the boy's transfer certificate. He's attending a new school this term.'

The trio goggled at this new information, as the principal leaned back in his chair, with an audible groan. The overhead tubelight showcased an oily sheen on his balding head.

'But sir–'

'I'm not saying I don't believe you. It was Mr Nagesh who recommended we print with Murugesh, last year. I'll put an end to that. I could give a police complaint for the damage in the shoproom, but regarding the leaking of question papers...' He shrugged, removed his glasses, and rubbed his face blearily.

'If you three are correct, then both problems of leaked question papers and stolen geometry boxes have been resolved, with both Ayyapan and Nagesh leaving school. If not, we will see. Either way, I don't want this matter pursued or discussed any further. I'll take it from here.'

The principal turned back to his computer. 'You may go back to class.'

✧

'You may go back to class,' grumbled Aarav in a mocking voice, as they walked back towards their blocks. 'Not even a thank you!' he shook his head in disgust.

'I'm just happy we solved the case first, rather than leave it to the grown-ups!' said Asha. She waved and skipped off to her class.

Aarav turned to Karthik. 'Don't you feel let down? If only we found a question paper, we would have had proof!'

Karthik shrugged. 'I'm not really disappointed. I don't think any of us wanted to see Ayyapan expelled.'

They stopped at the corner around Aarav's class. Karthik would have to go further down the corridor to reach his. Aarav nodded seriously. 'I guess it was lucky that Shop Uncle got him transferred.' He waved and disappeared around the corner.

Karthik watched him walk away thoughtfully, turned around, and headed away from his class.

CHAPTER 26

SECOND CHANCES

Entering the school shop, Karthik looked around cautiously. It was empty except for Shop Uncle, who glanced up from his paper, and grunted. 'I thought that little girl would be here first.'

'She's in class, but Asha's the one who figured it out.'

'Smart girl, that one.' Shop Uncle put his paper aside and folded his arms.

'Was it you?' Karthik ventured quietly.

'Me what?' countered Shop Uncle.

'Ayyapan was suddenly doing well. You must have wondered how.'

Shop Uncle leaned on his counter. 'Ayyapan studied hard and is now going to a better school.'

'Exactly. You got him transferred.' Karthik folded his arms, thinking hard. 'You must have known something was going on. Nuggets had fed him the questions papers. And then realized he could do this on a bigger scale. Through your other son's printing press.'

'I don't know anything about that. My son makes calendars.' Shop Uncle waved to the bird and tree calendar hanging up on the wall behind him.

'That's when Murugesh found out Ayyapan was cheating. Maybe Nuggets threatened to get Ayyapan expelled if they didn't cooperate?'

'I know my boys. They are both good and hard-working boys.'

'What I didn't get was what went wrong…' Karthik paced the shop, looking at all the notebooks, pencil boxes and other stationery stacked neatly in the shop. 'I thought it was an accident. Maybe you mixed up the boxes? Or sold them before Ayyapan came to help you?'

Shop Uncle reopened his newspaper with a snap, 'Did you want to buy something, *thambi*?'

Shaking his head, Karthik continued. 'But in hindsight, it was obvious.' Karthik pointed at the thick ledger on the counter. 'Asha mentioned you noted down everyone's name who bought another box.'

'I've been running this shop for thirty-six years, *thambi*. I remember my customers, and I always keep records.'

'You found it, didn't you? Boxes with question papers? The evidence.'

Shop Uncle smiled.

'And like any good father, or most fathers,' he amended, 'you were trying to protect them.' Karthik stopped pacing the shop and came to a halt in front of the owner and his register.

Shop Uncle came from around his counter and guided Karthik towards the door.

'I've seen lots of students come through these doors. Some steal, some lie, some cheat.' He shrugged again. 'As they grow they learn, as they learn they grow.'

He turned back to his shop, and added over his shoulder.

'But unlike the principal, I believe, everyone deserves second chances.'

CHAPTER 27

MR NOT-SO-PERFECT

'You could have at least told me!' huffed Aarav.

They were back in their clubhouse and Karthik was filling in the team about the final answers he got from Shop Uncle.

'I thought you didn't want to be the one doing all the talking, remember?' teased Karthik.

Karthik quickly raised two fingers up as a gesture of peace. 'Frankly, I wasn't sure. And I wanted to see his reaction.'

'But what I still don't get is the coupon error tagging.' asked Aarav.

'It's simple. The ones with the wrong award amount also carried the question papers to their buyers. And never were to be used in the contest. But…' Karthik held up a finger.

'Shop Uncle interfered!' Asha interrupted.

Karthik nodded seriously. 'I suspect he just opened every single box, pulled out any question papers he found, destroyed them, and then sold the boxes as usual. Not realizing they had been tagged.'

'And so Ayyapan is now frantically stealing back boxes, because if even one random person accidently found a question paper in the box, their game was up.'

'And Nuggets was obviously pissed and putting pressure on them both,' finished Aarav. 'Phew! What a case. No evidence and no arrest.'

'Oh, no...there is an arrest!' added Asha excitedly. 'Chicken Nuggets was caught trying to leave Bengaluru, apparently. Police uncle told me!' she smiled impishly, as the boys gaped at her.

'Well, then we are saved from Nuggets. I guess there will be a new PT teacher next term. We should celebrate that!' added Karthik.

'Hey, I nearly forgot!' Aarav finished his drink and tossed the empty bottle into the garbage. 'We've been asked to invite you for dinner tonight. My folks booked a place to celebrate their anniversary, and there are some minimum guest numbers. Our parents said to ask you,' Asha nodded along looking thoughtful.

‘Sure,’ said Karthik. ‘I’ll come. I wouldn’t want your guest count to be off,’ he added wryly.

‘Oh scratchmidget!’ yelled Asha smacking her forehead.

‘Is everyone stealing my word now?’ asked Aarav exasperatedly.

‘Our numbers were all wrong!’ Asha yelled at Karthik, ignoring Aarav.

Karthik froze. ‘What do you mean?’

‘We thought 100 boxes were tagged, but we were wrong. It was less, far less. And that’s why we

didn't find that many wrong coupons, when we did the second round.'

'No wonder, Murugesh was giving me a dirty look when I said I needed five coupons cause my friends had theirs stolen. He knew I was lying,' Karthik covered his eyes.

'It's far worse than that,' added Aarav gently.

Karthik uncovered his eyes.

'You've just ruined your perfect maths score!' Aarav guffawed and ducked as Karthik lobbed his pack of open chips at him.

ACKNOWLEDGEMENTS

In the beginning there was a word. And from those words came a story.

But embarrassingly enough, there was no one to listen to that story. And so this writer did what all writers do and bored her friends and family all about it.

That helped. Which is one reason why you now have this book in your hands.

The other reason is the incredible team at Scholastic, who believed in both the AKA series and this story, and brought it to life. Without my gung-ho editors, Prerna Mathur and Ashley Kumar, these words would have no form. Without illustrators like Charbak Dipta and designers like Niranjan Mishra, it would just be words without any of the exciting elements that help give your imagination a little nudge.

Without people like Shailee Chauhan and Sonal Grover, you would have never even known this book existed (much less decided to give it a read)! And without Madhumita Samantha, Shridhar Kulkarni, Vini Prasanna, and Archana, this book would not have reached your school, library, or neighbourhood bookshop.

And I know I'm missing many more. So suffice it to say, it takes a lot of work from many people, to get you a good book.

And I'm truly grateful.

Most authors also thank their readers on this page, (gold star if you've managed to keep reading till this point), but I'd like to thank your teachers and parents (or uncles, aunts, grandparents) who have put this book in your hands. You're amazing, keep doing it!

Finally, I want to thank my kids Diya and Nitin, and my husband Manoj Jacob for tolerating my writing storms which often come with thunder and sarcasm. It's part of my writing process. Sorry! And thank you.

About the Author

Based in Bengaluru, Vidya Varadarajan is a communications postgraduate with over 20 years of experience. Her career in advertising and digital marketing contributed to an early appreciation for the power of words.

Vidya believes in storytelling to bring forth honest conversations with children, and uses her writing to explore these themes. When not chasing her kids and their Lego-munching beagle, she pursues other creative passions including art, music, and gardening.

You can follow the author for her latest adventures on Instagram: @varadarajanv

BOOK 1 IN THE AKA SERIES: